Kid

My intention with this series of books is to understand and answer the questions about life posed by my boys. I have used my background as a licensed acupuncturist, diplomate of oriental medicine, biochemist and wife of a physicist who wrote his PhD thesis on the creation of the Universe.

My philosophy is to preserve health rather than to cure disease with the intention to help kids stay healthy and happy. Therefore, I would like to offer this guide to parents and kids on the human being as a whole, going into the macroscopic as well as the microscopic levels of life. The more kids know about their body, mind, and soul, the better they can take care of themselves.

Prevention starts at a young age, which is why I decided to make this information accessible to kids. Parents know their kids best, so the idea is that you use this book throughout your child's growth and adapt it to his or her knowledge and your background as your child grows.

Agnes Deglon
agnes@deglonconsulting.com

A big thank you to our reviewers and friends

For information contact Deglon Consulting LLC by mail or online:
Deglon Consulting LLC, P.O. Box 18538, Sarasota, FL 34276, USA.

www.KidsQuestionsAboutLife.com

The Journey of the Little Souls

Text and illustrations by Agnes Deglon
Edited by Patrick Deglon
Inspired by V. Deglon (age 4)

More information online at
www.KidsQuestionsAboutLife.com
www.facebook.com/KidsQuestionsAboutLife
www.twitter.com/kids_questions

Second Edition, February 2016

published by Deglon Consulting

Hi, I am Tony, a little bear and a being just like you. Did you know we are made of a body, a mind and a soul? I did not. I don't even know what these things are! So Mommy Bear and Daddy Bear tell me a lot about them. You want to know too? Then come join me on my journey! Let's take a look at the soul now.

Part 1

So I am a soul?
Wait . . . What does that mean?

These are the Teddys, Daddy Bear and Mommy Bear. Today Grandpa Bear is visiting. They have three kids, Big Sister Bear Vicky, Big Brother Bear Tony, and Baby Bear Charly.
The little ones are very curious and ask so many questions about the world, life, and just anything that crosses their minds.

Mommy and Daddy Bear do their best to answer them. Maybe you have similar questions, so the Teddys would like to share some of their answers with you.

Tonight, the Teddys are looking at the beautiful sky sprinkled with stars and a galaxy made from many, many stars. The little bears are very impressed.

Wow, Daddy Bear, what is all this? It's beautiful!

This is the Universe, the space we live in. The shiny dots are stars, little pieces of energy and matter floating around the Universe. I will tell you more about energy and matter in a little bit. The stars are very hot and bright. That's why you see them, and they are very, very far away, so they seem really small.

Grandpa Bear is also looking at the sky. He says he does it every night.
Grandpa Bear, what are you looking at?
See the little bright dots out there? I know they are stars, but I see them as little souls. I always look for Grandma's soul. You know, she died a little while ago. Her body is gone, but her soul is up there somewhere, waiting for me and everyone else she loves. I come to say hi to her every night, and she says hi to me too . . . Look! See the shooting star? I believe that's a sign from Grandma.

How did the stars get up there, Daddy Bear?

They are not really "up there." They are all around us, and we are part of all this. We are moving in space standing on a ball of matter, our planet Earth.

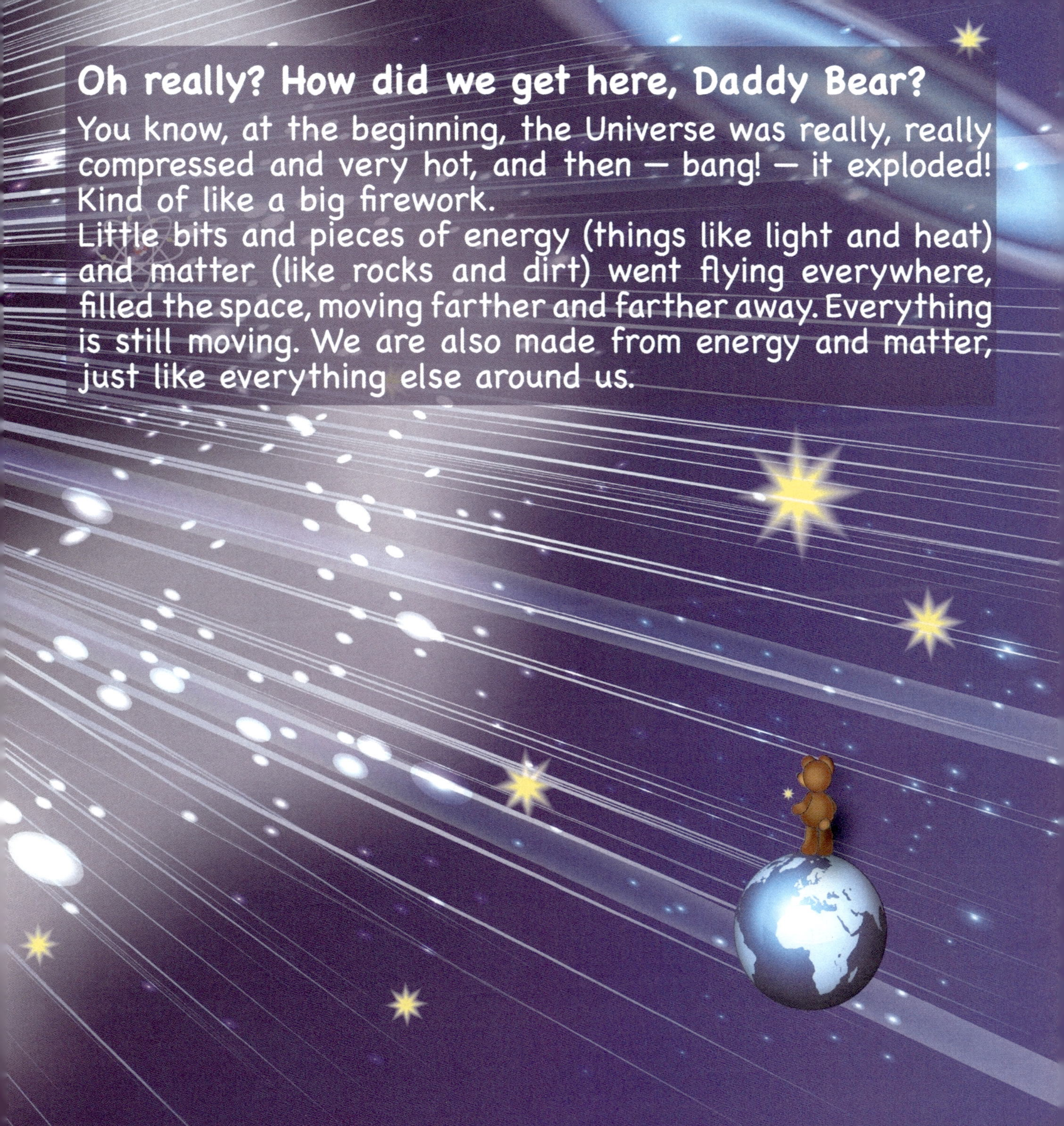

Oh really? How did we get here, Daddy Bear?

You know, at the beginning, the Universe was really, really compressed and very hot, and then — bang! — it exploded! Kind of like a big firework.

Little bits and pieces of energy (things like light and heat) and matter (like rocks and dirt) went flying everywhere, filled the space, moving farther and farther away. Everything is still moving. We are also made from energy and matter, just like everything else around us.

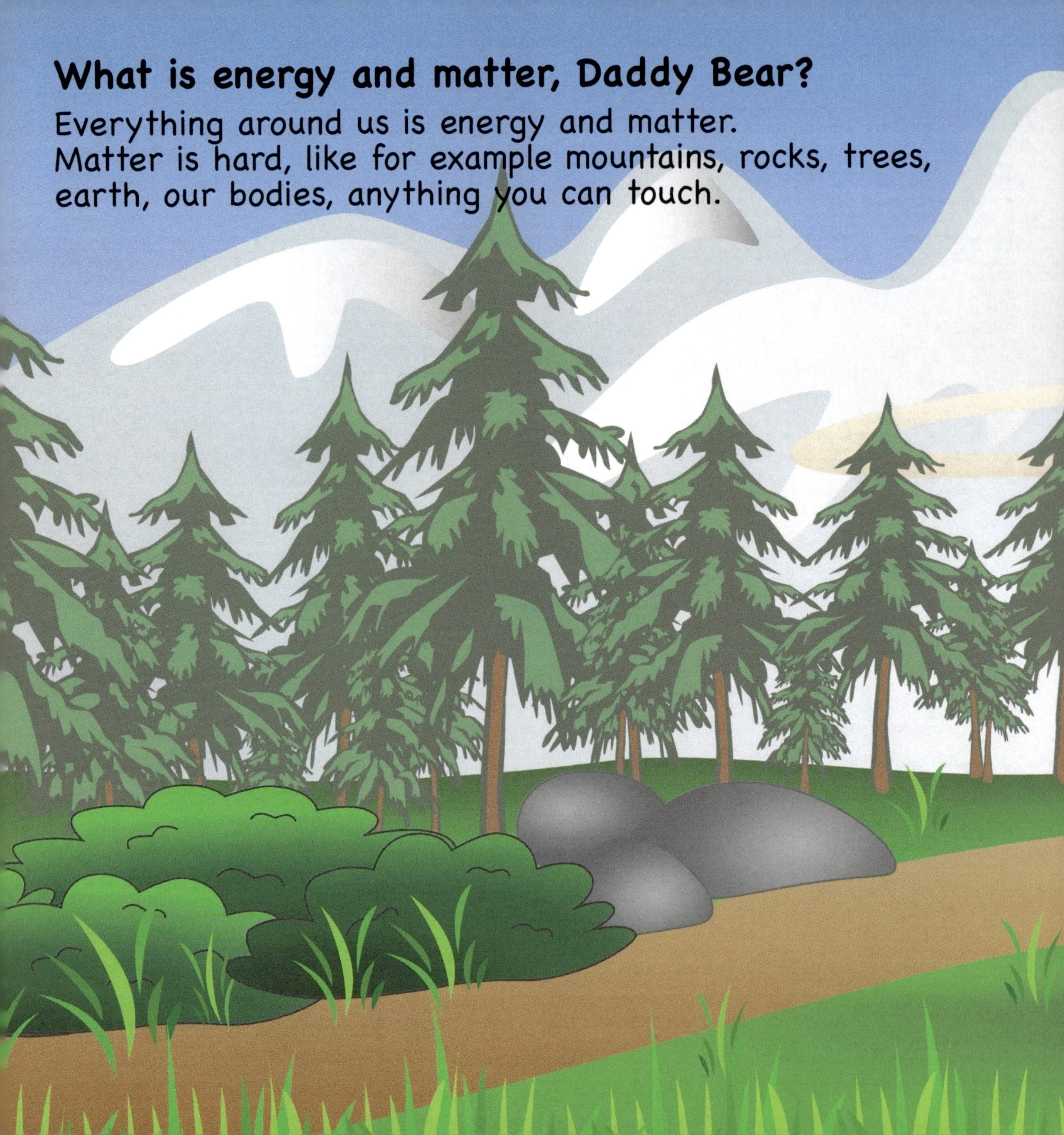

What is energy and matter, Daddy Bear?

Everything around us is energy and matter.
Matter is hard, like for example mountains, rocks, trees, earth, our bodies, anything you can touch.

Energy, you can't really touch, but you can feel it. For example, you can feel it as the heat or the movement of your body when you run, the light and warmth of the sun, or the love of a parent.

Our body is made from matter, but the energy in our body is what makes us alive.

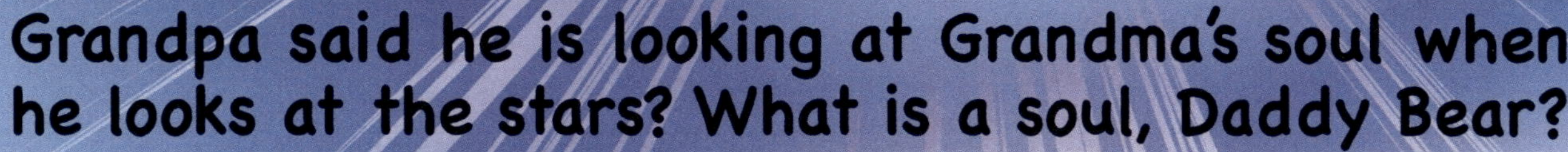

Grandpa said he is looking at Grandma's soul when he looks at the stars? What is a soul, Daddy Bear?

That's right, Grandpa feels the love from Grandma when he looks at the stars.
There is this big amazing, beautiful energy that fills us with warmth, love, happiness. We can call it the Divine Energy. Some people call it God, and other people use other words. It's all good. It is what makes us alive. We all carry a spark of this Divine Energy within us. We can call it our soul. This Energy never dies.

The next day the Teddy family is heading down to the ocean to visit Grandpa. He lives on his boat and the little ones love to go see him. On the way there, Vicky and Tony suddenly ask:

So we are energy and matter, Daddy Bear? Tell us more about it!

Yes, you are. Your body is matter, your soul is energy. To create life, energy needs to enter matter. Your soul enters your body. That's what makes you alive.

And then there is your mind*. It is also energy. It perceives the world around you (energy and matter) and stores memories. Body, mind and soul all work together. YOU ARE all these three things together!

* see book "Wait for me! Would you mind?"

The Teddys made it to the beach, and here comes Grandpa in his boat. Daddy Bear is still talking to the little bears.

Remember we talked about the Divine Energy and I said your souls are little sparks of this Energy? Look around you, see? Just like many stars form a galaxy, many droplets of water form an ocean, and many grains of sand form the beaches and deserts. Souls are connected and together they form the big Ocean of Souls, also called the Divine Energy.

So you and your friends are all just little parts of this big Ocean of Souls. Therefore, it is important to take care of your little friends and be nice to each other. We are all little droplets of the same ocean. We are the same energy, the Divine Energy.

Grandpa is connected to Grandma through this loving energy.

Daddy Bear, how did my soul get into my body?

That happens as Mommy and Daddy make a baby. Remember how your body is made in Mommy's belly from Daddy Bear and Mommy Bear's cells*? The cells join together and then start to divide into more and more cells to form the baby's body.

* see book "Hey Buddy, I am your Body!"

The little souls that form the big Ocean of Souls feel the energy of love from Mommy and Daddy when they make the baby. One soul will be drawn into the bundle of cells that grows in Mommy's belly to form a new baby — its new body.

The little souls come into our bodies to spend time on Earth, which is a world of solid matter. Remember, the little souls are energy, so they are a bit like bubbles, very airy and light. The world of solid things is very different from them.

While a soul is in a body, it gets to experience the world. It gets to use the body's senses to experience things like the beauty of nature, the taste of strawberries, the smell of fresh baked cookies, the sound of music, the touch of furry animals, or it gets to play and touch sand, water, plants, mud . . . Those are the more concrete parts of life on Earth.

The Teddys are tired after the long hike, and the night comes quickly. After a nice dinner on the beach with Grandpa, they all go to sleep. Grandpa says good night to Grandma and goes to sleep on his boat. The others sleep under the palm trees on the beach.
The night is quiet, the sky full of stars.
Everyone is sleeping happily . . . or almost.

Tony is happily exploring the world of dreams . . . flying around and having fun.

What are dreams, Daddy Bear ?

The world of dreams is where the little soul goes on many adventures. When the body is asleep, the little soul can go on a journey.

In our dreams, we can do whatever we want. We can build sandcastles on the beach, swim in the ocean, fly with the birds.

We can roll around in the snow and build a snow-teddy or play hide-and-seek in the green forests. Anything is possible . . . and Tony is having fun!

Vicky is having less fun. Her dreams are scary and dark. She needs some help to be reassured and go back to sleep safely.

Why do I have nightmares, Mommy Bear ?

Aw, I know, that's scary. Sometimes the little soul runs into "bad guys" or "bad thoughts" on its journeys. It gets scared. The beautiful dreams can turn into nightmares.

What are "bad" guys and "good" guys, Mommy Bear?

You know, every soul is good, but some people's thoughts and actions are bad. Bad thoughts lead to bad actions, and that happens if you don't listen to your soul. "Bad" guys are souls in bodies that are frustrated and unhappy because their minds are telling them to do things that don't feel right.

Sometimes, all it takes to turn them into "good" guys is to find the reason why they are unhappy. We should try to understand them, help them find what they need by reminding them to listen to their souls.
All of us can do good and bad things sometimes.

I am going to tell you a little secret, so listen carefully: You can protect yourself from bad dreams by blowing your soul into a bigger and bigger bubble of light, love, and energy until you are completely surrounded by this bubble and you feel safe. Bad guys and bad thoughts don't like love and light. They won't come near you in your bubble of light, or if they do, they will become light and love themselves. But this needs some practice. So close your eyes and imagine your soul getting really big around you. Sleep soundly and without fear now, my baby girl! Remember, our souls are sparks of Divine Energy. It will always be there to protect us.

The next morning they wake up to discover that Grandpa is not waking up.
The little bears are very sad, they love their Grandpa and don't understand.

Daddy Bear, why is Grandpa not waking up?

You know, our bodies all die at some point. Grandpa was very old, he spent a lot of time on Earth. His body did not work very well anymore, so his soul left. What you need to know is that dying is not an end but a transformation. However, it is still sad for the families and friends left behind.

They say Grandpa died from something called . . . death! Yes, that's what they say. It is when you get super old, and then one night, you fall asleep, and then the next morning, you wake up dead . . . Actually, just your body is dead, your soul is not! Souls don't die. They are energy. Energy does not die, right, Vicky?
That's right, Tony! When the body does not wake up, they say you are dead! But I don't think this is really the end. Do you?

Daddy Bear, what happens when we die ?

In the body, the little soul has a lifetime to experience life on Earth. One day, when the little soul leaves, the body will be dead, it will return to dust*. The little soul will go back to spend time with its friends, the other little souls. The little soul will feel happy and at peace within the big Ocean of Souls and the Divine Energy.

* see book "Hey Buddy, I am your Body"

Daddy Bear, can I hug Grandpa ghost?

Hmm . . . You can feel him, but you can't touch him anymore. Ghosts are airy like little souls. They have left their earthly bodies, but they have not yet been able to go back to their friends in the Ocean of Souls.

Why are you still here, Grandpa Bear?

I still have a few things to finish, Tony. I need to give you the key to my boat before I leave, so you can sail it now. I can't take it with me. Souls don't need boats or keys or any material things.

And I feel held back on Earth by your soul in your earthly body. I know you don't want me to go, but it is time for me now. I need to get back to Grandma's soul and the other souls out there, we need to say goodbye for now little bear. Meet me at night where I used to say hi to Grandma, ok?

But Daddy Bear, why do some souls leave their body when they are still very young?

That is a very difficult question little bears. I am afraid I don't have the perfect answer for you. Remember when we talked about the body*? I said that some day everybody will die. When the body gets to the point where it is either too old or too sick or too broken, it can't heal itself anymore. That's when the little soul leaves.
But never forget, little bears, even when the body dies, the soul never does. Its energy and love will always be with us.

* see book "Hey Buddy, I am your Body"

Now every night, the little bears go to say good night to the souls of Grandpa and Grandma Bear, just like Grandpa did for many years with Grandma.

Part 2

So souls are coming and going. Why?

Maybe, one day Grandpa's soul will come back in another baby's body, so it can live another beautiful and enriching lifetime. Some people believe souls come back; others think they don't. It is all okay. You believe what feels right for you.

This is so cool! It is like every time I come to Earth, I get a new vehicle! This time, I am driving a car, and next time, I get to drive a big truck. Maybe next time, I get to fly an airplane, and next time, I am the captain of a boat or an astronaut in a spaceship. . . and so I get to discover the world from many different places. That is really awesome! What are you going to drive in your next lifetime, Vicky?
Hmmm, I don't care too much about vehicles. I would like to ride horses, have my own pets, and grow my own garden with fruits, berries, veggies.
I don't think you have to wait a lifetime for that, Vicky. Want to go to the farm now?

Why are the souls coming to Earth in our bodies, Daddy Bear?

Each time a soul enters a body to spend a lifetime on Earth, it has a purpose. The difficulty can be to find or remember this purpose.

Only you can know what your purpose is in this lifetime. In order to find out, you could try sitting down in a quiet place. Close your eyes and connect to your soul and the Divine Energy. This is called meditation. Sit and listen — or actually, I should say feel — feel what is coming to you. You will know when your soul talks to you because it will just feel right.

Keep asking the question, "What is my purpose of life?"

Sitting and listening is just one way to find out about your purpose of life. There are many ways a message can come to you. Just stay open and receive, anytime, anywhere.

We may all have different purposes in life; however, what we have in common is that we are all part of the big Ocean of Souls. So be aware that the answer has a bigger goal, a goal to make the world a better place for everybody. It is not a selfish goal. It is about helping everyone, about improving things, feeling good, and making others feel good. Since we are all part of the same whole, helping others is helping ourselves too.

Hey Tony, what are you doing here?
Good question Vicky! I am here... hmmm... to figure out what I am doing here?! Meanwhile I am looking at the shooting stars!
I am here to teach my students!
I take care of people!
I make clothes!
I take care of nature!
I am here to grow food for every-one!

We are all here to help make the world a better place. Some of us may be here to build homes, others to take care of nature, to keep things clean, or to help people stay healthy.

I like to keep things clean and tidy!
I am a gardener, and I love nature!
I love people, so I do my best to help!

Others are teaching and learning. Students learn from the teacher, and teachers learn from the students.

Some prepare food for others. Some have fun sewing and making clothes.

Our goal here is to help you find your true path, to help you stay happy and healthy, to feel good in your body. And your job is to keep looking for your answer, the one that feels right for you.

When you get off track you will start to feel frustrated, unhappy, or sick. And that will happen. It happens to everybody at some point. It's okay. Just do your best to get back on track.

Remember, you will know when your soul is talking to you because it will just feel right. Only you will know. No one else can tell you. You may not know immediately, and that's fine too. You can get there little by little. As long as you are on the right path, you will feel happy, peaceful, excited, just good!

You will notice little signs in your life coming from the Universe. It is up to you to discover those signs.
Open your eyes to see, open your ears to hear,
Open your nose to smell, open your mouth to taste, open your hands to touch, and open your heart to feel and love.
Enjoy your journey, little souls!

Hey, I am Grandpa's energy. I don't have a body anymore. I just used this shape so that you can recognize me. But I am here to help you. I always have been here, and I always will!

About the Author

Agnes Deglon holds degrees in subjects ranging from translation to biochemistry. Not just satisfied with the scientific approach to life, the author seeks to further explain the Universe.

Through her studies in the Eastern approach to medicine and the body, mind, soul connection, Agnes has rounded out her understanding and approach to that which is not taught in schools but is required for a healthy and happy life.

This endeavor became even more important to her after her first child started questioning the Universe and asked the question that many parents fear: "What's a soul?"

With a loving approach and scientific structure, Agnes is writing a trilogy of critical books. Her new series *Kids' Questions about Life*, is a crucial guide to the human being. Body, mind and soul are explained in the children's own language.

If you liked my book,
like me on Facebook
www.facebook.com/
KidsQuestionsAboutLife

This book is part of a trilogy about body, mind and soul.

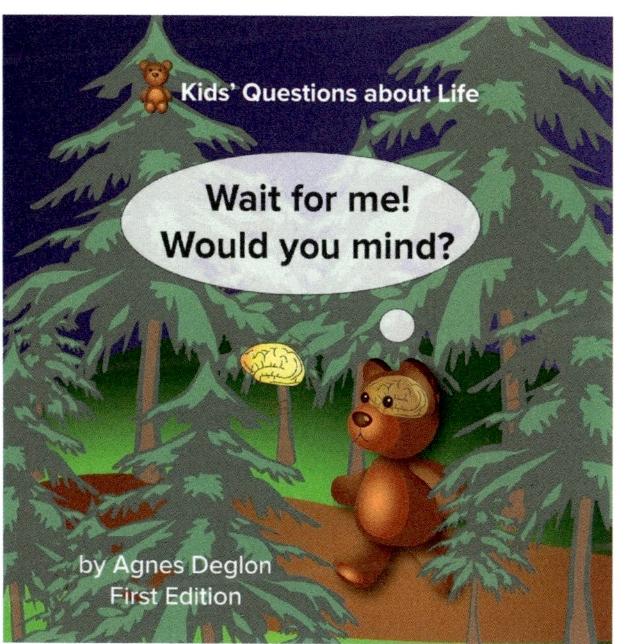

You can find more information online at

www.KidsQuestionsAboutLife.com

Sign-up online to stay up-to-date with our latest books and products.

Made in the USA
Charleston, SC
27 April 2016